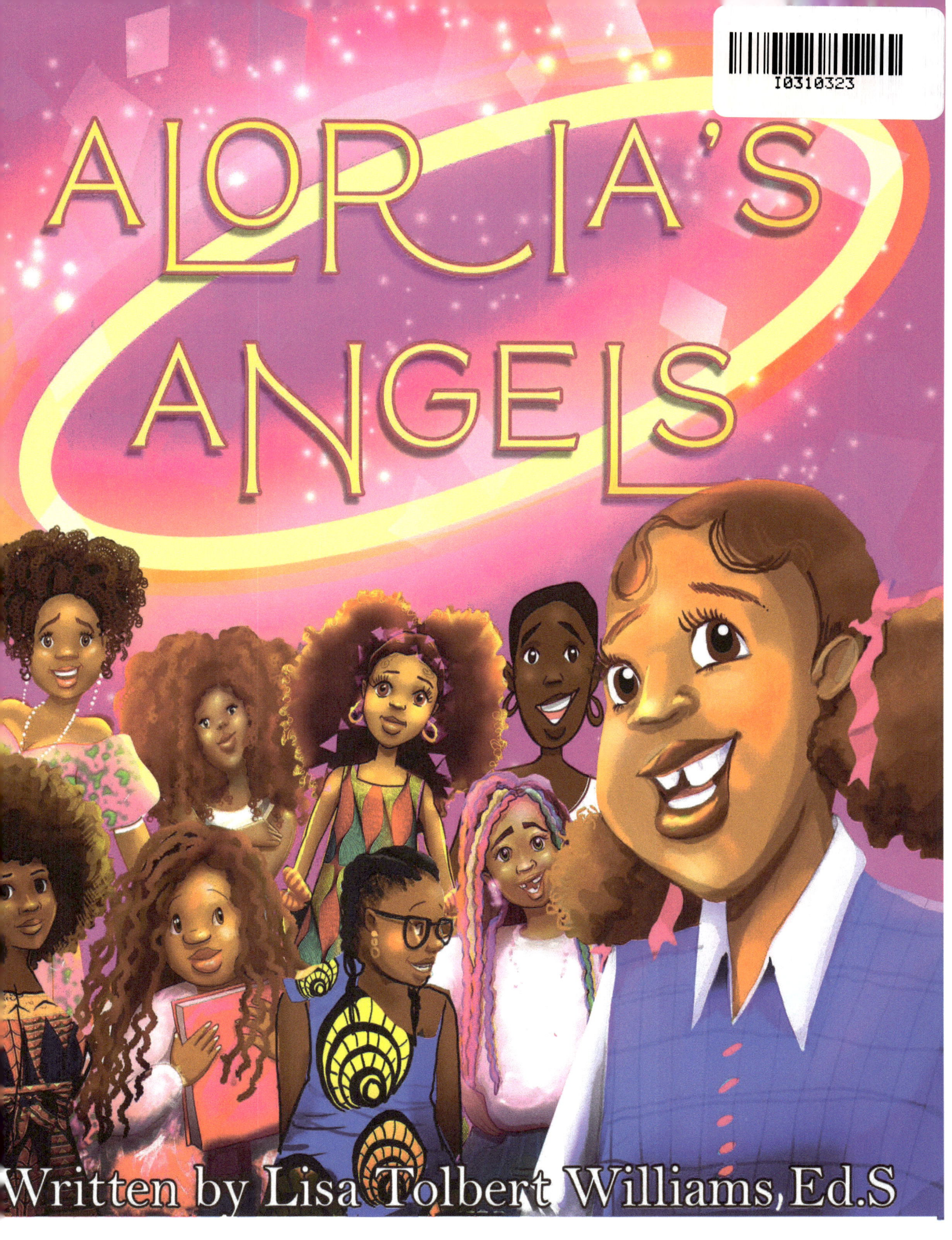

Aloria's Angels by Lisa Tolbert-Williams, Ed.S

© 2022 Lisa Tolbert-Williams, Ed.S

Published by
Lisa Tolbert-Williams, Ed.S

Edited by Lisa Tolbert-Williams, Ed.S and Angie Rhodes-Cato

All rights reserved. No part of this publication may be reproduced, distributed, or transmitted in any form or by any means, including photocopying, recording, or other electronic or mechanical methods, without the prior written permission of the publisher, except in the case of brief quotations embodied in critical reviews and certain other noncommercial uses permitted by copyright law. For permission requests, write to the publisher, addressed "Attention: Permissions Coordinator," at the address below.

Aloria's Angels
P.O. Box 1876
Jonesboro, GA 30236

Email: aloriasangels@gmail.com

Web address: www.aloriasangels.com or www.lisatolbertwilliams.com

ISBN:978-0-578-35385-2
Audience: Ages 3 - 12
1. Children 2. Education 3. Picture Book 4. Easy Readers

Printed in the United States of America

This book is in memory of the following Heavenly Angels

Ethel McCants Tolbert, Grandmother
Elizabeth Tolbert Goins, Aunt
Nellie Mae Tolbert Thornton, Aunt
Roxie Tolbert McNiel, Aunt
Sarah Pearl Scott, Aunt
Frances Williams, Aunt

A special thank you to
Marcus Williams, Nubian Bookstore
Gwendolyn-Glenda Tolbert Dailey, Mother
Mary Bertha Anderson, Aunt
Callie Cooper, Aunt
Marion Williams, Aunt
Hazel Clements, Aunt
Family & Friends

www.lisatolbertwilliams.com

Gloria's Angels

www.lisatolbertwilliams.com

This book belongs to:

_____

www.lisatolbertwilliams.com

LEETHA

THALI

LIZZIE

ALORIA

TOLLIE

www.lisatolbertwilliams.com

My name is ───────────────────

My birthday is ─────────────────

I am ──────── year old

My favorite color is ─────────────

My favorite food is ──────────────

I like to ──────────────────────

I am good at ──────────────────

Some words that describe me are: ────
───────────────────────────────

I AM AWESOME BECAUSE...

I AM WORTHY

THALI

www.aloriasangels.com

5

www.lisatolbertwilliams.com

I AM WORTHY BECAUSE...

_____
_____
_____
_____
_____
_____
_____
_____
_____
_____
_____

I HELP OTHERS BECAUSE...

I AM SMART

LIZZIE

www.aloriasangels.com

www.lisatolbertwilliams.com

I LOVE MYSELF

CHAN

www.aloriasangels.com   21

ANYTHING IS POSSIBLE

FRANCIE

www.gloriasangels.com

ANYTHING IS POSSIBLE BECAUSE...

I AM IMPORTANT

LEESAH

www.aloriasangels.com

www.lisatolbertwilliams.com

I AM IMPORTANT BECAUSE...

ALORIA'S ANGELS CERTIFICATE

This certificate certifies that

_____

Student Name/ New Angel

Has completed all the affirmations and is now a member of

ABOUT THE AUTHOR

Lisa Tolbert Williams, Ed.S is an HBCU Graduate of Alabama State University. She received a Bachelors of Science (2000) Major: Computer Information Systems and Marketing from Alabama State University. Later, she received a Master of Arts in Special Education (2006) from The University of West Florida. Lastly, she received an Education Specialist Degree in Technology Management Administration(2008) from Nova Southeastern University.

Lisa believes that life is full of dreams, visions, affirmations, angels, and most of all love. She has thousands of stories to unfold and millions of young readers to inspire. Her hobbies are reading, writing, cooking, and traveling the world. Her passion is to make you smile when you purchase a publication from Lisa. Her life motto is simple "Angels are everywhere".

Stay tuned young readers. She has many more publications to publish. Find her via web:

 @AloriasAngels, @Lisa Tolbert Williams #AloriasAngels, #LisaTolbertWilliams

 Lisa Tolbert Williams #LisaTolbertWilliams #AloriasAngels

 @LisaTolbertWilliams, #AloriasAngels, #LisaTolbertWilliams

 @AloriasAngels, @Lisa Tolbert Williams #AloriasAngels, #LisaTolbertWilliams

 Lisa Tolbert Williams

www.lisatolbertwilliams.com

www.ingramcontent.com/pod-product-compliance
Lightning Source LLC
Chambersburg PA
CBHW061759290426
44109CB00030B/2898